HALLOWE COOKBOOK FOR KIDS

FUN HALLOWEEN RECIPES FOR KIDS

CONTENTS

HALLOWEEN COOKBOOK FOR KIDS

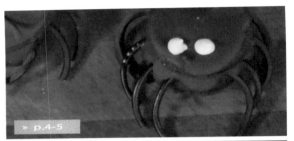

» p.4-5

» p.8-9

» p.16-17

» p.25_25

» p.32-33

» p.36_37

CHOCOLATE SPIDER COOKIES

CHOCOLATE SPIDER COOKIES

DIRECTIONS

1. Melt the chocolate chips in a heatproof bowl over a pan of simmering water. Once the chocolate has melted turn the heat off but keep the bowl over the water to keep the chocolate warm while you assemble the spiders.

2. Cut the liquorice laces into 3cm lengths, these are going to be the spiders legs. You will need 96 lengths in total for all the spiders legs.

3. Place a small teaspoon of melted chocolate into the middle of an Oreo cookie. Stick 8 liquorice legs into the chocolate, then sandwich a 2nd Oreo cookie on top of the first.

4. Cover the top of 2nd Cookie with chocolate and place on a baking sheet to set.

5. Once the chocolate has set use the white and black icing pens to make eyes on the spiders.

Prep time	Cook time	Ready in	Serves
15 min	10 min	35 min	12

INGREDIENTS

- 12 packs Oreo cookies
- 1 cup milk chocolate chips
- 1 pack liquorice laces
- White and black icing pens

CHOCOLATE MONSTER COOKIES

DIRECTIONS

1. Make the chocolate filling:
2. Heat the cream in a medium saucepan on a medium heat until it boils. As soon it boils remove from the heat.
3. Immediate add the milk chocolate and stir with a silicone whisk. Once the chocolate and cream have combined stir in the butter. You should have a smooth mixture. Cool in the fridge for 3 hours until set.
4. Assemble the Monster cookies:
5. Spread the chocolate filling over half of the cookies. Make the filling thicker on one side of the cookie. This will make it look like the monster is opening its mouth when the other cookie goes on top.
6. Place the other half of the cookies on top at a slight angle to get the monster effect.
7. Cut 20 small triangles out of mini marshmallows, put on the thicker bit of the chocolate filling to look like teeth. Put 2 teeth on each monster.
8. Use the vanilla frosting to attach the white chocolate buttons for eyes, use a black icing pen to draw on pupils. Keep in the fridge until ready to serve.

Prep time	Cook time	Ready in	Serves
15 min	15 min	30 min	10

INGREDIENTS

- 2 packs soft bake chocolate chip cookies (20 cookies)
- 20 white chocolate buttons
- 1 ½ cups milk chocolate chips
- 1 cup cream
- 2 tablespoon unsalted butter
- Handful of white marshmallows
- ¼ cup vanilla frosting
- Black icing pen

DIRECTIONS

1. Make the brownies according to the directions on the pack, in a 10½" x 8" tin.

2. Once the brownies have cooled cut into 12 pieces. Put on a wire rack with a greaseproof lined metal sheet underneath to catch the frosting drips.

3. Using a small amount of vanilla frosting stick a marshmallow to the top of each brownie.

4. Pour over the rest of the frosting onto the marshmallows. The marshmallows should be completely covered and the frosting should drip slightly onto the brownies. If the frosting is too thick to pour you may need to add a very small amount of water to get it to pouring consistency.

5. Once the frosting is completely dry use the black icing pen to decorate with ghostly faces.

GHOSTLY BROWNIES

Prep time	Cook time	Ready in	Serves
15 min	20 min	35 min	12

INGREDIENTS

- 1 pack of brownie mix
- 12 large white Marshmallows
- 1 cup vanilla frosting
- Black icing pen

MINI PUMPKIN PIZZA

DIRECTIONS

1. Preheat the oven to 350°F. Line 2 baking sheets with baking parchment.

2. Prepare the toppings. Thinly slice the olives and cut the salami slices into triangles.

3. Put the flour tortillas on the prepared baking sheets, thinly cover the tortillas with pizza sauce.

4. Cover all of the pizza sauce layer with cheese.

5. Decorate with olives or salami triangles to create the pumpkin look. Place a basil leaf at the top of the tortilla for the stem.

6. Cook for around 5-7 minutes in the oven, or until the cheese is melted and golden brown.

MINI PUMPKIN PIZZA

Prep time	Cook time	Ready in	Serves
15 min	20 min	35 min	6

INGREDIENTS

- 1 pack flour tortillas
- 8oz pizza sauce
- 8oz grated orange cheddar cheese
- 6 fresh basil leaves
- Black olives and salami slices (to decorate)

DIRECTIONS

1. Melt the chocolate in a heatproof bowl over a pan of simmering water. Once melted turn off the heat but keep the bowl over the pan to keep warm.
2. Prepare a wire rack with a greaseproof lined baking sheet underneath to catch the chocolate drips.
3. Dip the doughnuts into the melted chocolate. Use a cocktail stick to help turn the doughnuts in the chocolate, then remove and place on the wire rack. While the chocolate is still wet place 2 M&Ms on the side of the doughnut, these will be the eyes.
4. Allow the chocolate to set for around 1 hour, the chocolate should be slightly firm but not solid.
5. Get 80 pretzel twists and cut each in half to give you 160 half moon shapes. These will be the spiders legs. Add 8 pretzel legs to each spider by pushing the half moons into the top of the chocolate doughnuts.
6. Use the black icing pen to draw pupils onto the eyes. Leave to set for at least 3 hours.

MINI DOUGHNUT SPIDERS

Prep time	Cook time	Ready in	Serves
15 min	20 min	35 min	20

INGREDIENTS

- 1 box mini doughnuts
- 1 cup milk chocolate chips
- 1 pack large pretzel twists
- Handful M&Ms
- Black icing pen
- Cocktail sticks

DIRECTIONS

1. 1. Melt the chocolate in a heatproof bowl over a pan of simmering water. Once melted turn off the heat but keep the bowl over the pan to keep warm.
2.
3. 2. Prepare 2 baking sheets lined with baking parchment. Dip each strawberry in the white chocolate and leave to set on the baking sheet. Try to get a bit of a drip underneath the strawberry as this make them look more ghostly.
4.
5. 3. If using chocolate drops to decorate make the ghosts faces immediately while the chocolate is still wet. Set in the fridge for at least 1 hour.
6.
7. 4. If decorating with a black icing pen do this once the chocolate has set.
8. .

GASTLY STRAWBERRIES

Prep time	Cook time	Ready in	Serves
15 min	20 min	35 min	20

INGREDIENTS

- 1 punnet of strawberries (washed)
- 1 cup white chocolate chips
- Dark chocolate chips or black icing pen

EYEBALL SOUP

DIRECTIONS

1. First prepare the eyeballs. Drain the mozzarella balls then, using a small melon baller, scoop out a hole from each mozzarella ball.

2. Halve each pimiento-stuffed olive.

3. Place an olive half, cut-side-out, in the hole in each mozzarella ball to make eyeballs.

4. Prepare soup according to directions on the can.

5. 5. Ladle hot soup into bowls and carefully float 4 or 5 eyeballs in soup. For the best effect use large, shallow bowls.

6. Add edible blood to the eyeballs for extra goriness and season with salt and pepper.

EYEBALL SOUP

Prep time	Cook time	Ready in	Serves
10min	15 min	20 min	6

INGREDIENTS

- 1 can Campbell's condensed tomato soup (10 ¾oz)
- 30 mini mozzarella balls
- 1 jar small pimiento stuffed olives
- Salt and pepper to season
- Edible blood

DIRECTIONS

1. Melt the chocolate in a heatproof bowl over a pan of simmering water. Once melted turn off the heat but keep the bowl over the pan to keep warm.

2. Use a small amount of melted white chocolate to attach the M&Ms to the top of the marsh-mallows. Leave to set for 1 hour.

3. With the red icing pen draw veins on the eyeballs, coming out from the M&M pupil and down the side of the marshmallow.

4. Dip the bottoms in edible blood before serving, for extra effect serve the eyeballs on a shallow plate of edible blood.

BLOODY MARSHMALLOW EYEBALLS

Prep time	Cook time	Ready in	Serves
15 min	20 min	35 min	30

INGREDIENTS

-
- 30 white marshmallows
- 30 blue and green M&Ms
- ½ cup white chocolate chips
- Red icing pen
- Edible blood

DIRECTIONS

1. Prepare a wire rack with a greaseproof lined baking sheet underneath to catch the frosting drips. Arrange the mini doughnuts on the rack with around 1cm between each doughnut.

2. Put the vanilla frosting into a jug and pour over the top of the doughnuts. You may need to add a very small amount of water to get the frosting to a pouring consistency.

3. While the icing is still wet put an M&M in the middle of each doughnut. Leave to dry for at least 2 hours.

4. Decorate with the red icing pen, draw veins on the eyeballs, coming out from the M&M pupil and down the side of the doughnuts.

SCARY DOUGHNUT EYES

Prep time	Cook time	Ready in	Serves
15 min	20 min	35 min	20

INGREDIENTS

- 20 mini doughnuts
- 1 cup vanilla frosting
- Red icing pen
- 20 blue & green M&Ms

BANANA GHOSTS

DIRECTIONS

1. Push the ice pop stick into the cut end of each banana half. Freeze for at least 2 hours until firm.

2. Line a large baking sheet with baking parchment, make sure there is room for the sheet to lie flat in the freezer.

3. Melt the white chocolate in a heatproof bowl over a pan of gently simmering water. Once the chocolate has melted turn the heat off but keep the bowl over the water to keep the chocolate warm.

4. Dip the frozen bananas into the white chocolate, use a spoon to cover the bits that may have been missed when dipping.

5. While the chocolate is still wet press mini chocolate chips into chocolate to create eyes and faces.

6. Place coated bananas on greaseproof lined sheet to set. Freeze for at least 4 hours, up to 1 week.

BANANA GHOSTS

Prep time	Cook time	Ready in	Serves
15 min	10min	25min	8

INGREDIENTS

- 4 bananas, peeled and halved
- 8 ice pop sticks
- 3 cups white chocolate
- Handful mini chocolate chips

DIRECTIONS

1. Put the gelatin powder into a small bowl then add the boiling water. Once dissolved add the 2 packs of jello and stir until fully dissolved.
2. Once the mixture has cooled to room temperature add the whipping cream and 1 teaspoon green food coloring.
3. Pull the straws straight with the flexible bit fully extend. Fully open or cut off the top your empty carton, you should have a tall rectangular box (make sure it has been washed out)
4. Pack as many straws as you can fit into the carton without squishing the straws. The flexible ends of the straws should go in the bottom of the container (upside down straws).
5. Add the jello mixture to the straw filled container, fill to just below the top of the container. Set in the fridge overnight.
6. Just before serving run the worms under hot water and they should slide out.
7. Serve on a plate of crushed up Oreos to look like dirt.

WIGGLY BOWL OF JELLO WORMS

Prep time	Cook time	Ready in	Serves
15 min	20 min	35 min	12

INGREDIENTS

- 2 packs raspberry jello
- 1 packet unflavored gelatin powder
- 3 cups boiling water
- ¾ cup whipping cream
- Green food coloring
- Pack of flexible straws
- Tall container to put straws in (empty 1 litre carton of juice or milk works well)
- 1 pack crushed Oreos

DIRECTIONS

1. Put all ingredients in a bowl (except for the corn starch) and mix to a smooth paste.

2. If you would like to thicken the blood sieve in a teaspoon of cornstarch, whisk rapidly as you add it to get rid of any lumps.

CHOCOLATE SPIDER COOKIES

Prep time	Cook time	Ready in	Serves
-	-	5 min	-

INGREDIENTS

- 1 large tablespoon corn syrup
- 1 large tablespoon maple syrup
- 1 teaspoon red food coloring
- Few drops blue food coloring
- Corn starch (optional)

BANANA GHOSTS

DIRECTIONS

1. Place the eggs in a single layer in a large saucepan. Pour water over the eggs to cover, then add the 3 tablespoons of blue food coloring to the pan.

2. Bring pan to the boil and simmer for 3 minutes. Leave eggs to cool in the liquid for 10 minutes.

3. Remove the eggs from the pan with a slotted spoon and place on folded dishtowel to dry. Do not throw away the cooking liquid.

4. Lightly crack the egg shell with a wooden spoon, this will create the spider web pattern on the side of the eggs.

5. Once all eggs have been cracked, place them in a bowl and cover with the cooking liquid. Leave to cool in the refrigerator.

6. Peel shells from the eggs just before serving, season with salt and pepper.

SPOOKY SPIDERWEB EGGS

Prep time	Cook time	Ready in	Serves
5 min	3 min	10 min	12

INGREDIENTS

- 1 dozen large eggs
- Blue food coloring
- Salt and Pepper to serve

FRANKENSTEIN CUPCAKES

DIRECTIONS

1. Make up the cake mix according to the directions on the pack, divide between the 12 muffin cases. You need the cupcakes to rise slightly above the edges of the muffin cases for this recipe to work well so add slightly more mixture to each muffin case than normal. Bake according to the pack directions.

2. Once the cakes have cool cut 2 semi circles from the left and right edges of each muffin leaving a 1-inch rectangular raised cake platform in the middle of the muffin. This rectangle will be Frankenstein's face.

3. Add a few drops of green food coloring to the vanilla frosting to get a Frankenstein green colour. Carefully cover the top of the cakes with the green frosting. Place a marshmallow on either side of the cake rectangle at the bottom. These will be Frankenstein's neck bolts.

4. Leave to dry for at least 2 hours. Decorate faces onto the Frankenstein's with the black and white icing pens.

Prep time	Cook time	Ready in	Serves
10 min	20 min	2 hours	12

INGREDIENTS

- 1 pack vanilla cake mix
- 12 muffin cases
- 1 cup vanilla frosting
- Green food coloring
- Handful white mini marshmallows
- Black and white icing pens

DIRECTIONS

1. Make up the cookies according to the pack instructions. Bake the cookie dough into bat shapes.

2. Mix the vanilla frosting with 2 teaspoons of black food coloring, add more if needed to make a dark black colour. Spoon the frosting into the piping bag and cut a small hole in the bottom.

3. Ice the bodies of the bats then cover completely in chocolate vermicelli. Leave to dry for 30mins, shaking lightly to remove the excess vermicelli. Fill in the wings with the rest of the black frosting in the piping bag. Set aside the leftover black icing for later.

4. Use the white icing pen to dot 2 eyes onto each bat. Once the eyes have dried dot on a small black pupil with a cocktail stick using the leftover black frosting.

SPOOKY BAT BISCUITS

Prep time	Cook time	Ready in	Serves
15 min	20 min	35 min	6

INGREDIENTS

- 12 packs Oreo cookies
- 1 cup milk chocolate chips
- 1 pack liquorice laces
- White and black icing pens

DIRECTIONS

1. Place the popping corn and vegetable oil in a large pan over a medium heat. Stir to coat in oil.
2. Once the kernels start to pop place a lid on top of the pan, then turn the heat down to low.
3. Shake the pan while cooking to stop the popcorn sticking or burning, hold the lid firmly on. Do this until the kernels have stopped popping, around 5 minutes.
4. Tip the popcorn into a large bowl and discard any unopened kernels.
5. Heat the butter and marshmallows in saucepan over a low heat until melted. Pour this mixture over the popcorn and mix well.
6. Lightly oil your hands and shape the popcorn into small brain shaped balls. Leave on a baking parchment lined baking sheet to set.
7. Once set draw a red line down the middle and veins over the brains with the red food coloring and paintbrush. Splatter with edible blood to serve.

BRAINBALLS

Prep time	Cook time	Ready in	Serves
15 min	20 min	35 min	20

INGREDIENTS

- 170g popping corn
- 2 tablespoons vegetable oil, plus extra for shaping
- 50g butter
- 170g marshmallows
- Red food coloring
- Small paintbrush
- Edible blood

DEVILLED EYEBALLS

Prep time	Cook time	Ready in	Serves
15 min	20 min	35 min	20

DIRECTIONS

1. Peel the cooled hard-boiled eggs, then cut in half lengthwise. Carefully remove the yolks and put in a medium sized bowl, arrange the egg whites on a serving platter.

2. Cut the avocados in half, remove the stone and scoop out the flesh to add the bowl of yolks. Add the lemon juice, salt and pepper to the bowl then mash this mixture with a fork until smooth.

3. Fill the empty egg white halves with the avocado mixture, pile it high to look like the iris of an eyeball. Add a slice of olive to the centre of the avocado mixture for the pupil.

4. Finally mix the mayonnaise with 1 teaspoon of red food coloring, or until you have made a blood red colour. Carefully spoon this mixture into the piping bag and cut a small hole in the bag. Decorate the eyeballs with blood red veins.

INGREDIENTS

- 10 hard-boiled eggs
- 2 ripe avocados
- 1tablespoon lemon juice
- ½ teaspoon salt
- ½ teaspoon ground black pepper
- 5 black olives
- 3tablespoon mayonnaise
- Red food coloring
- 1 disposable piping bag

DIRECTIONS

1. Remove the string cheese from the plastic wrap and cut each string cheese into 3 equal pieces.

2. Pull apart the string cheese to make it look like a broomstick end. Don't pull all the way to the top of the cheese pieces or the broomstick ends will fall apart.

3. Carefully push a pretzel rod into each string cheese.

4. Decorate using a fresh chive, tie the chive around the string cheese near to the pretzel end.

CHEESY BROOMSTICKS

Prep time	Cook time	Ready in	Serves
15 min	20 min	35 min	20

INGREDIENTS

- 1 pack string cheese
- 1 pack pretzel rods
- Handful of fresh chives

EYEBALL CAKE POPS

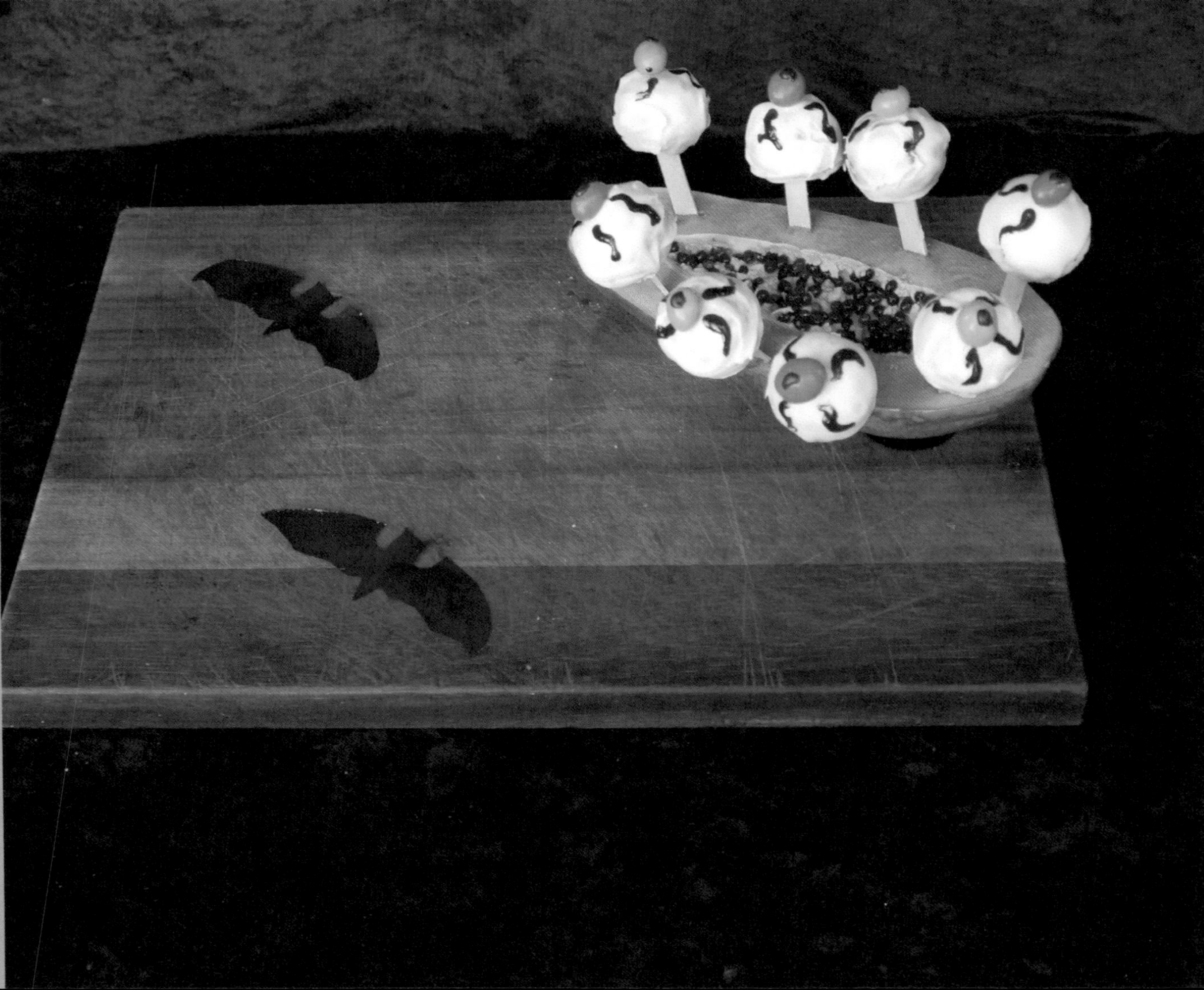

DIRECTIONS

1. Melt the milk chocolate in a heatproof bowl over a pan of simmering water.

2. Break the sponge cake and cookies into a food processer, add the melted milk chocolate and pulse to combine into a smooth mixture.

3. Tip the cake mixture into a bowl, use your hands to make into walnut sized balls. You should make around 10. Place on baking sheet lined with baking parchment and chill in the fridge for 2 hours until firm.

4. Melt the white chocolate in a heatproof bowl over a pan of simmering water. Once melted turn off the heat but keep the bowl over the water to keep warm.

5. Remove the balls from the fridge and place a skewer in each ball. Spoon over the white chocolate until completely covered.

6. Stand the coated cake pops in the pumpkin and press an M&M onto the side of the balls. Chill in the fridge until the chocolate has set. Once set use the icing pens to add a pupil and wiggly red veins to make the cake pops look like eyeballs.

EYEBALL CAKE POPS

Prep time	Cook time	Ready in	Serves
15 min	20 min	35 min	10

INGREDIENTS

- 4oz vanilla sponge cake
- 1 pack Oreo cookies
- ½ cup milk chocolate chips
- ½ cup white chocolate chips
- Blue and green M&Ms
- Red and black icing pens
- 10 wooden skewers
- 1 small pumpkin (to serve)

DIRECTIONS

1. Make up the cookies according to the pack instructions. Bake the cookie dough into circles around 3 inches in diameter.

2. Once the cookies have cooled ice the top of all the cookies with a thin layer of vanilla frosting.

3. Use the black icing pen to pipe a circle at the outer edge of the cookies. Leave a small gap and pipe another circle inside this circle, repeat this until you can't fit any more circles on the cookie.

4. While the frosting is still wet use the cocktail stick and pull through the black circles to the centre of the cookies, this should give a spider web patter. Decorate the cookies with the spider decorations.

SPIDERWEB COOKIES

Prep time	Cook time	Ready in	Serves
15 min	20 min	35 min	6

INGREDIENTS

- 1 pack vanilla sugar cookie mix
- Vanilla frosting
- Black icing pen
- Mini spider decorations
- Cocktail stick

DIRECTIONS

1. Before cooking the hot dogs use a knife to cut markings into them to make them look like fingers. Three lines across the middle and 2 lines ¾ way up should look good. Cut way a small flat square section at the tip to leave space for the fingernail.
2. Cook hotdogs according to the pack instructions.
3. Cut the hotdog rolls in half, put a large blob of ketchup in one end and spread halfway down the bun. You should leave half the bun sauce free for the best effect.
4. Put the cooked hotdogs into the buns, with the non-fingernail end sitting in the ketchup end of the bun.
5. Cut the onion in half and separate the layers, cut out fingernail shapes from the layers, before adding to hot dogs put a little dot of ketchup underneath the fingernail and let the ketchup squeeze out a bit.
6. 6. Finally put some more ketchup on the bloody end of the finger and splash the buns and hot dogs with edible blood.

BLOODY HOT DOG FINGERS

Prep time	Cook time	Ready in	Serves
15 min	20 min	35 min	12

INGREDIENTS

- 12 large hot dogs
- 12 hot dog buns
- 1 large onion
- Ketchup
- Edible blood

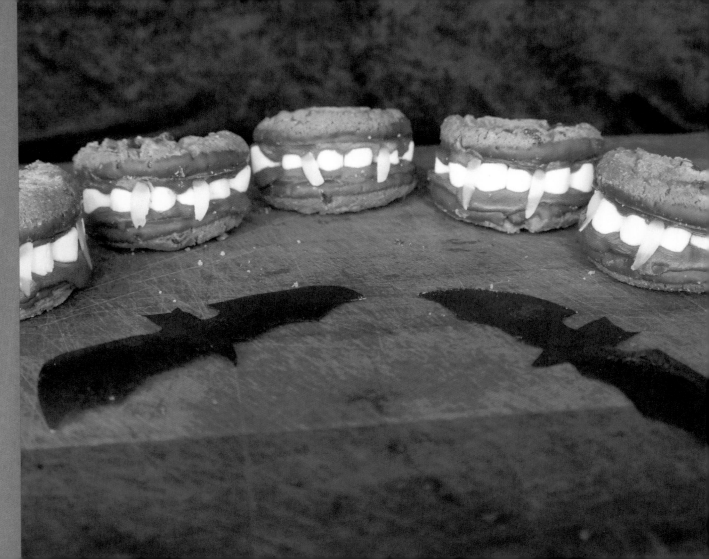

DIRECTIONS

1. Prepare the cookies as directed on the packet to make 24 cookies.

2. After removing cookies from the oven, leave to cool for 2mins, then cut each cookie in half (cookies are easier to cut while still warm). Move cookie halves to wire rack to cool completely.

3. Mix the vanilla frosting with the red food coloring to make a red colour for the gums.

4. Spread a layer of the red frosting onto the bottom side of all the cookie halves.

5. On 12 of the cookie halves place a ring of 6 marshmallow teeth. Place an extra marshmallow behind these to help support the cookie.

6. Place the remaining 12 cookie halves onto the marshmallow bases.

7. Cut the sliced almonds into small slivers, and place 2 almonds in between the teeth for fangs. You can dip the tip of each almond sliver into frosting to help them stick.

DRACULA'S DENTURES

Prep time	Cook time	Ready in	Serves
15 min	20 min	35 min	24

INGREDIENTS

- 1 pack chocolate chip cookie mix (18.25oz)
- ½ cup vanilla frosting
- 2 cups mini marshmallows
- Handful sliced almonds
- Red food coloring

DIRECTIONS

1. Put all the ingredients except for the almonds into a food processer. Pulse until the mixture comes together, but the mixture is still has some texture.

2. Line a baking sheet with baking parchment. Mold the mixture into finger shapes and place on the sheet.

3. Push an almond onto the tip of each finger to look like a fingernail. Put the sheet into the fridge to set for at least 1 hour and up to 1 day.

4. Serve the fingers poking out of a bowl.

ZOMBIE FINGERS

Prep time	Cook time	Ready in	makes
15 min	20 min	35 min	10-15

INGREDIENTS

- 1 cup stoned dates
- ½ cup dark chocolate chips
- 3 tablespoon smooth peanut butter
- 3 tablespoon porridge oats
- Handful flaked toasted almonds

DIRECTIONS

1. Preheat the oven to 350°F. Line a cupcake tin with cupcake cases.

2. In a medium bowl mix together the flour, salt and spices.

3. In a large bowl whisk together both sugars, butter and eggs. Add the flour mixture to this bowl and whisk until smooth. Finally whisk in the pumpkin puree.

4. Divide the mixture evenly between the cupcake cases, about halfway full. Bake for about 20-25 minutes until cake tester comes out clean.

5. Transfer to a wire rack to cool.

PUMPKIN CUPCAKES

Prep time	Cook time	Ready in	makes
15 min	20 min	35 min	18

INGREDIENTS

- 2 cups self-raising flour
- 1 teaspoon salt
- 1 teaspoon cinnamon
- 1 teaspoon ground ginger
- ¼ teaspoon freshly grated nutmeg
- ¼ teaspoon ground allspice
- 1 cup light brown sugar
- 1 cup granulated sup
- 1 cup unsalted butter, melted and cooled
- 4 large eggs
- 1 can pumpkin puree (15 ounces)
- Vanilla frosting
- Halloween cupcake decorations

SCARY BREADSTICK SNAKES

DIRECTIONS

1. Preheat the over to 350°F. Line 2 baking sheets with baking parchment.
2. Unroll the refrigerated pizza dough and cut into 12 strips.
3. Roll each strip into a 12-inch long rope shape. Make one end pointed (for the tail) and one end larger and flattened (to create the head).
4. Wrap each rope around a greased chopstick into a spiral and place on the baking sheet. Brush the snakes with olive oil. Sprinkle the body with poppy seeds and cover the tails with sesame seeds.
5. To make the eyes cut black olives into small triangles, place on the head of the snakes. Cut the sundried tomatoes into tongue shapes, save for once the snakes have been cooked.
6. Bake for 15-20mins, until golden brown. While the snakes are still warm use a cocktail stick to make a small hole in the head of the snake and add the sundried tomatoes to look like tongues.

SCARY BREADSTICK SNAKES

Prep time	Cook time	Ready in	Serves
15 min	20 min	35 min	12

INGREDIENTS

- 1 tube refrigerated pizza dough (14oz)
- 2 tablespoons poppy seeds
- 1 tablespoon sesame seeds
- 1 tablespoon olive oil
- Handful of black olives
- Handful sundried tomatoes
- 12 greased chopsticks

DIRECTIONS

1. Follow the instructions of the pack to make the lime jelly.

2. Pour ½ of the jelly mixture into the chosen serving pots, add a couple of jelly sweets to each container. Put the pots into the fridge to set and leave the rest of the jelly mixture at room temperature.

3. Once set add the other ½ of the jelly mixture to the pots and add some more jelly sweets to the pots. Lean some of the sweets against the edges to make the stick out the top of the jelly. Put back in the fridge to set.

4. To make the soil topping put the Oreo cookies into a food processor and pulse until large crumbs (soil consistency).

5. Just before serving sprinkle a layer of the Oreo soil on top of each set jelly and then top with a selection of creepy crawlies.

SLIME BUG CUPS

Prep time	Cook time	Ready in	makes
15 min	20 min	35 min	12

INGREDIENTS

- 2 packs of lime jelly
- 2 packs Oreo biscuits
- Selection of animal and bug jelly sweets
- 12 small glasses or plastic pots for serving

DIRECTIONS

1. Beat the butter and sugar together in a large bowl until light and fluffy. Then beat in the egg, almond extract and vanilla extract until well combined. Mix in the flour and salt and bring together to form a dough. Cover the bowl with plastic wrap and cool in the fridge for 1 hour.

2. Preheat the oven to 350°F. Take the dough out of the fridge and prepare a baking sheet by lining with baking parchment.

3. To shape the fingers roll out to about the size of an adults pinkie, then add an almond to the tip for a fingernail, pressing down firmly to ensure it's secure. Squeeze the finger to form a knuckle and use a knife to make some creases on the fingers.

4. Place the shaped fingers on the baking sheet about 1cm apart. Chill for 20mins. Bake for 15-20mins, or until lightly golden. Cool on a rack.

5. Once the fingers have cooled remove the almond from the fingertip, add a small amount of jam into the area where the

SEVERED FINGERS

Prep time	Cook time	Ready in	makes
15 min	20 min	35 min	20

INGREDIENTS

- 1 cup butter
- 1 cup powdered sugar
- 1 egg
- 1 teaspoon almond extract
- 1 teaspoon vanilla extract
- 1 ½ cups plain flour
- ½ teaspoon salt
- ½ cup blanched almonds
- 1 cup strawberry jam

almond would have been, then put the almond back. Make sure you put enough jam to ooze out the side a bit. Dip the other end of the finger in the jam, and add some round the knuckles for extra effect.

6. Place the remaining jam in a small ramekin for a dip and arrange the fingers around this on a large plate.

MUMMIFIED FRANKFURTERS

DIRECTIONS

1. Preheat the oven to 350°F. Line 2 baking sheets with baking parchment.

2. Unroll the pizza dough and cut into 12 equal strips. Roll each strip into a thin 20-inch long rope shape.

3. Starting at the bottom of the frankfurter wrap the pizza dough rope around the frankfurter to look like a mummy. ¾ of the way up leave a gap for the eyes. Cut the strip here, then use the remaining bit of the strip to wrap the top of the frankfurter.

4. Place the wrapped frankfurters on the prepared baking sheets.

5. Bake for 15-20mins until golden brown, use the cocktail stick to dot on eyes with mayonnaise. Serve immediately with ramekins of ketchup and mustard.

MUMMIFIED FRANKFURTERS

Prep time	Cook time	Ready in	Serves
15 min	20 min	35 min	6

INGREDIENTS

- 1 tube refrigerated pizza dough (14oz)
- 12 frankfurter sausages
- 1 tablespoon mayonnaise
- Cocktail stick
- Ketchup and mustard

DIRECTIONS

1. Melt the milk chocolate in a heatproof bowl over a pan of simmering water.

2. Break the sponge cake and cookies into a food processer, add the melted milk chocolate and pulse to combine to a smooth mixture.

3. Tip the cake mixture into a bowl, use your hands to make into golf ball sized pieces. Shape these pieces into mouse shapes and roll in cocoa powder. Add almonds for ears and liquorice laces for tails

4. Place on sheet lined with baking parchment and chill in the fridge for 2 hours until firm.

SCARY CHOCOLATE MICE

Prep time	Cook time	Ready in	makes
15 min	20 min	2.5 hours	6-8

INGREDIENTS

- 4oz vanilla sponge cake
- 1 pack Oreo cookies
- ¼ cup sour cream
- ½ cup milk chocolate chips
- ½ cup cocoa powder
- Handful silver dragees (edible silver balls)
- Sliced almonds
- 1 pack liquorice laces

DIRECTIONS

1. 1. Chop the onions into small pieces, add to a large pan with the garlic and the oil. Sautee on a medium heat for around 5 minutes.

2. 2. Add the pumpkin, chicken stock and thyme. Bring to the boil, reduce heat to low and simmer for around 30 minutes, until the pumpkin has softened.

3. 3. Remove the pan from the heat and use a stick blender to puree the soup until smooth.

4. 4. Cut the top of the serving pumpkins, scoop out the seeds then rinse out. Return the pan to the heat, add the cream and season with salt and pepper.

5. 5. Pour into the prepared pumpkins just before serving.

PUMPKIN SOUP

Prep time	Cook time	Ready in	Serves
15 min	20 min	35 min	8

INGREDIENTS

- 1 teaspoon vegetable oil
- 3 crushed garlic cloves
- 2 large onions
- 6 cups chicken stock
- 4 cups fresh pumpkin
- Handful fresh thyme
- ½ cup cream
- Salt and pepper to season
- 2 medium pumpkins to serve

Printed in Great Britain
by Amazon